M000049778

RED HOT
SRIRACHA

50 RECIPES

THAT WILL KICK YOUR ASS!

MELISSA PETITTO

Race Point
PUBLISHING

Race Point Publishing
An imprint of Quarto Publishing Group USA Inc.
276 Fifth Avenue, Suite 205
New York, NY 10001

RACE POINT PUBLISHING and the distinctive Race Point Publishing logo are trademarks of
Quarto Publishing Group USA Inc.

Photography by Bill Milne (except as noted below)
Food Styling by Justin Nilson
Cover design by Heidi North
Interior design by Marc Cohen

Cover photo (flames/dragon) © Shutterstock
Chili peppers illustration (top of each page)© Shutterstock
Clock face illustration (page 7) © Getty Images (Artist: Dorling Kindersley)
Fork and spoon illustration (page 19) © Getty Images (Artist: Dorling Kindersley)
Appetizers illustration (page 45) © Shutterstock
Chef's hat illustration (page 65) © Shutterstock
Slice of pie with cherry illustration © Shutterstock
Corn illustration © Shutterstock
Drink illustration © Shutterstock
Chili, Garlic, and Ginger Sautéed Greens (page 94) © Shutterstock
Peanut Butter Chocolate Chip Cookies (page 104) © Shutterstock
Falafel with Tahini Sauce (page 96) © Shutterstock

ISBN: 978-1-631060-48-9

Library of Congress Cataloging-in-Publication Data is available

Printed in China

10 9 8 7 6 5 4 3 2 1

CONTENTS

INTRODUCTION

Oh, sriracha, most versatile and beloved of all condiments! You are worshipped and revered. You alone are my faithful companion on this journey to making good food taste even better.

When I began developing recipes for *Red Hot Sriracha*, I knew I couldn't do it alone. *Everyone* loves sriracha. How could I possibly accommodate all the varied uses for this indispensable condiment? So I asked friends, family, random strangers, "what do you put sriracha on?" The answers I got were as varied and incredible as the Thai spicy chili paste itself. Vegetarians use it to kick up the flavor in some of their veggie-based dishes. Take-out lovers drizzle it on their Chinese and Thai. Meat lovers marinate their cuts in the delectable hot sauce. I met people who add it to breakfast foods, cocktails, shots, and even desserts. I incorporated many of these ideas when developing the recipes you see here, and the others came from some of my own secret uses for sriracha (addicts never tell). I hope you enjoy them, and by all means, send me your creative uses for sriracha, too, since I clearly can't get enough.

The heat scale I used throughout the book (indicated at the top of each recipe and iconically represented by a chili pepper) is a 1 to 5 rating system, with 5 being the spiciest. Don't think a 5 is hot enough for you? You can absolutely increase the spice level of any beverage, dish, or appetizer simply by adding a little or a LOT more sriracha to it. Get ready for some satisfied taste buds (if you haven't destroyed them yet, of course).

As a personal chef, I tend to create and use recipes that are simple and straightforward. I don't fuss with a lot of esoteric ingredients, and I firmly believe that fresh, wholesome ingredients are the way to go—it's the best way to maximize your flavor…and your sriracha. I think the one item you might not have lying around your kitchen is a donut pan, but believe me those Sizzling Chili and Lime Donuts (see page103) are worth the purchase of one!

Special thanks to John Clift, state ambassador for Jackie O's Brewery in Athens, Ohio. This amazing man helped me develop the spicy cocktails in the Drinks chapter (see page 111) and all I can say is wow. My mouth is still burning!

All right, folks, it's about to get hot in here…

—*Melissa Petitto*

SPICY BAKED HUEVOS RANCHEROS

Skip buying hordes of spices to make an "authentic" Mexican dish. Instead, play it like a pro by combining store-bought enchilada sauce with sriracha for an instant fix that's the cornerstone of this morning casserole.

INGREDIENTS

Cooking spray, for greasing

12 fresh corn tortillas

2 teaspoons sea salt, divided

1 15-ounce can red enchilada sauce

½ cup (120ml/4fl oz) sriracha, plus more for serving

1 cup (115g/4oz) shredded pepper jack cheese

1 (15-ounce) can refried black beans

8 large eggs

1 teaspoon freshly ground black pepper

½ cup (8g/¼oz) cilantro, chopped

2 avocados, sliced

2 limes, quartered

½ cup (120ml/4fl oz) sour cream

COOKING INSTRUCTIONS

1. Preheat the oven to 375°F (190°C). Grease an 11 x 13-inch (28 x 33cm) baking dish and set aside.

2. On a baking sheet, arrange the corn tortillas in a single layer and sprinkle with 1 teaspoon salt. Bake for 8 to 10 minutes, or until crispy and lightly browned. Allow to cool slightly, then tear or break each tortilla into quarters. Set aside.

3. Combine the enchilada sauce with the sriracha in a small bowl and stir until blended. Set aside.

4. To assemble the casserole, arrange half of the tortillas in a single layer in the prepared baking dish. Top with half of the enchilada-sriracha sauce, followed by half of the cheese, then all of the refried beans. Repeat the layers of tortillas, sauce, then cheese.

5. Carefully crack the eggs on top of the casserole, spacing them evenly across the surface. Season with the remaining 1 teaspoon salt and pepper.

6. Bake until the eggs are fully set but the yolks are still runny, about 20 to 25 minutes. Watch the casserole closely for around 20 minutes to ensure you don't overcook the eggs.

7. To serve, sprinkle with cilantro and serve with avocado slices, lime wedges, sour cream, and extra sriracha.

EGG, POTATO, AND CHORIZO SIZZLER

Two tablespoons of sriracha may seem a little light-handed for one whole dish, but when it's combined with ground chorizo sausage (go for extra hot!), you're looking at a double-fisted sucker punch of spice.

INGREDIENTS

4 medium red-skinned potatoes, quartered

2 tablespoons olive oil, divided

2 tablespoons sriracha, divided

1 teaspoon smoked paprika

¾ teaspoon sea salt, divided

½ teaspoon freshly ground black pepper

1 red, green, or yellow bell pepper, seeded and diced

1 medium onion, diced

1 pound (450g) spicy chorizo sausage, removed from casings

4 large eggs

1 large tomato, diced, for serving

¼ cup (60ml/2fl oz) sour cream, for serving

¼ cup (15g/½oz) parsley, chopped, for serving

Toasted bread, for serving (optional)

COOKING INSTRUCTIONS

1. Preheat the oven to 425°F (220°C). Line a baking sheet with aluminum foil and set aside.

2. In a medium bowl, combine the quartered potatoes, 1 tablespoon olive oil, 1 tablespoon sriracha, paprika, ½ teaspoon salt, and pepper. Toss to coat. Transfer to the prepared baking sheet and roast for 15 to 20 minutes, or until golden and crispy. Set aside.

3. While the potatoes are roasting, heat the remaining 1 tablespoon olive oil in a large sauté pan over medium heat.

4. Add the bell pepper and onion and sauté for 5 minutes, or until softened and lightly browned. Add the chorizo and cook for an additional 8 minutes, breaking up the sausage with a wooden spoon.

5. While the sausage cooks, lightly whisk the eggs in a medium bowl and season with the remaining 1 tablespoon sriracha and ¼ teaspoon salt.

6. Push the chorizo mixture to the side of the sauté pan. Add the eggs to the pan and scramble for 2 to 5 minutes, or until they reach the desired doneness. Mix the eggs into the chorizo mixture.

7. Add the roasted potatoes to the pan and stir to combine.

8. To serve, spoon the scramble onto plates and top with diced tomato, sour cream, and chopped parsley. Serve with toast if desired.

EGGS IN A FIERY HOLE

Your favorite childhood breakfast is grown up and kicking ass in a corner office. It's all about the thick, spongy brioche and fiery pepper sauce, with its tangy-hot mix of sriracha, basil, vinegar, and Dijon.

INGREDIENTS

CHILI SAUCE
1 16-ounce jar roasted peppers, drained
¼ cup (60ml/2fl oz) sriracha
¼ cup (6g/¼oz) basil leaves
1 tablespoon olive oil
1 tablespoon red wine vinegar
1 teaspoon Dijon mustard
¼ teaspoon sea salt

2 tablespoons salted butter
4 slices brioche bread, 1 inch (2.5cm)
   thick
4 large eggs
1 teaspoon sea salt, divided
1 teaspoon freshly ground black pepper,
   divided
Cilantro, for garnish

COOKING INSTRUCTIONS

1. To make the chili sauce, combine the roasted peppers, sriracha, basil, olive oil, red wine vinegar, Dijon, and salt in a food processor. Process on high for 1 minute, or until smooth. Set aside.

2. Heat a large sauté pan or griddle pan over medium heat. Melt the butter.

3. While the pan is heating, use a biscuit cutter or the rim of a glass to cut a hole in the center of each slice of bread.

4. When the butter has melted, place the slices of bread in the pan and crack an egg into the center of each hole.

5. Cook until the eggs set a bit on the bottom, about 1 minute. Sprinkle the eggs with half the salt and pepper.

6. Flip each slice and season the reverse side with the remaining ½ teaspoon each salt and pepper. Cook for an additional 1 to 2 minutes, or until the yolk has reached your desired degree of doneness and the bread is golden and toasted.

7. To serve, spread the chili sauce on four plates, top with the egg in a hole, and garnish with cilantro.

EGGS IN PURGATORY

You could call this a spicy spin on shakshuka—or, better yet, just a damn easy way to get perfect eggs every time. Bonus: Everything's cooked in one pan, making prep and cleanup that much easier.

INGREDIENTS

¼ cup (60ml/2fl oz) olive oil
3 jalapeños, stemmed, seeded, and finely chopped
1 onion, diced
4 garlic cloves, minced
1 teaspoon ground cumin
1 tablespoon smoked paprika
1 28-ounce can crushed tomatoes with juice

½ cup (120ml/4fl oz) water
¼ cup (60ml/2fl oz) sriracha
1 teaspoon sea salt
4 large eggs
½ cup (85g/3oz) sheep's milk feta cheese, crumbled, for serving
1 tablespoon parsley, chopped, for serving
Warm pita, for serving

COOKING INSTRUCTIONS

1. Heat the olive oil in a large sauté pan over medium-high heat.

2. Add the jalapeños and onion and cook, stirring occasionally, for about 6 minutes, or until softened and golden brown.

3. Add the garlic, cumin, and paprika and cook, stirring frequently, for about 1 minute, or until the garlic is fragrant.

4. Add the tomatoes, water, and sriracha and bring to a boil. Reduce the heat to low and simmer for 15 minutes, or until thickened. Season with salt.

5. Crack the eggs on top of the sauce in the pan, spacing them evenly across the surface. Cover the pan and cook for 5 minutes, or until the yolks are just set.

6. Sprinkle with feta and parsley and serve with pita for dipping.

CHILI CHICKEN AND WAFFLES

Serves 4

Marinating your chicken in buttermilk before frying? Hello, amateur hour. Grow a pair and bathe it straight-up in sriracha. Push things even further with a sriracha-laced waffle batter and finishing syrup.

INGREDIENTS

CHICKEN

¼ cup (60ml/2fl oz) sriracha

¼ cup (60ml/2fl oz) water

1 cup (125g/4½oz) all-purpose flour

1 teaspoon sea salt

1 teaspoon freshly ground black pepper

1 teaspoon garlic powder

4 boneless, skinless chicken breasts,
    cut in half

1 cup (235ml/8fl oz) vegetable oil

1 teaspoon Maldon Flaked Sea Salt

WAFFLES

2 cups (250g/9oz) all-purpose flour

3½ teaspoons baking powder

½ teaspoon sea salt

2 large eggs

1½ cups (355ml/12fl oz) buttermilk

¼ cup (60g/2oz) unsalted butter, melted
    (½ stick)

½ cup (120ml/4fl oz) sriracha

SRIRACHA MAPLE SYRUP

1 cup (235ml/8fl oz) maple syrup

1 cup (235ml/8fl oz) sriracha

COOKING INSTRUCTIONS

1. Preheat the oven to 200°F (90°C). Fit a baking sheet with a wire rack and set aside.

2. Whisk together the sriracha and water in a medium bowl and set aside.

3. In a large zip-tight plastic bag, combine the flour, salt, pepper, and garlic powder and mix well.

4. Dip each chicken breast into the sriracha sauce until coated and let any excess liquid drip off. Place each breast, one at a time, into the bag of seasoned flour. Seal the bag and shake to coat evenly. Transfer the coated chicken breast to a plate, then repeat with the remaining chicken.

5. Heat the vegetable oil in a large, deep skillet over medium-high heat until the oil reaches 350°F (180°C).

Instructions continued on next page

CHILI CHICKEN AND WAFFLES

Continued

COOKING INSTRUCTIONS

6. Carefully add the chicken and fry, until golden brown, about 5 to 7 minutes. Flip the chicken over and fry for another 5 to 7 minutes, or until golden brown on both sides and the meat is cooked through. Transfer to the prepared wire rack and sprinkle with Maldon Sea Salt: Place chicken in the oven to keep warm.

7. To prepare the waffles, first preheat a waffle iron and lightly grease.

8. Whisk together the flour, baking powder, and salt in a large bowl.

9. In another large bowl, whisk together the eggs, buttermilk, melted butter, and sriracha. Add the wet ingredients to the dry ingredients and mix until just absorbed. The batter will be very thick and fluffy.

10. Scoop ½ cup (120ml/4fl oz) batter into the hot waffle iron and cook until golden brown and lightly crisp. Lightly cover the cooked waffles to keep warm while making the remaining waffles.

11. To prepare the sriracha maple syrup, in a medium bowl, whisk together the maple syrup and sriracha. Set aside.

12. To serve, top each waffle with some chicken and drizzle with sriracha maple syrup.

SOUPS

CHILI TOMATO BREAD SOUP

Can peasant food be sexy? Well, it is now, because we're all up in this rustic soup's business. Bright and lush, it's a clever twist on traditional Italian bruschetta or panzanella.

INGREDIENTS

¼ cup (60ml/2fl oz) olive oil, plus extra
  for drizzling

1 small sweet onion, diced

6 garlic cloves, minced

1 28-ounce can diced plum tomatoes
  with juice

2 tablespoons tomato paste

¼ cup (60ml/2fl oz) sriracha, plus
  extra for drizzling

1½ teaspoons sea salt

1 teaspoon freshly ground black pepper

4 cups, or 1 quart, (950ml/32fl oz)
  chicken or vegetable broth

1 pound (450g) stale country bread,
  crust removed and cut into cubes
  (about 8 cups)

½ cup (12g/½oz) basil leaves, plus
  extra for garnish

COOKING INSTRUCTIONS

1. Heat the olive oil in a large Dutch oven over medium heat.

2. Add the onion and cook, stirring occasionally, for about 5 minutes, or until translucent.

3. Add the garlic and stir for 1 minute, or until fragrant.

4. Add the diced tomatoes, tomato paste, sriracha, salt, pepper, and broth. Increase the heat to high and bring to a boil. Reduce the heat to a simmer and cook for 10 minutes, stirring occasionally.

5. Add the bread cubes and basil. Stir and mash the bread to absorb the liquid.

6. For a chunky, rustic soup, serve as is. For a creamier texture, transfer to a blender and blend until smooth.

7. To serve, ladle the soup into bowls, then drizzle with olive oil and sriracha and top with torn basil leaves.

THAI CORN CHOWDER

It's OK to get a little handsy with the spice in this dish. Add an extra glug of sriracha into the corn mixture, or maybe swizzle some on top of the finished soup. It's only gonna get better.

INGREDIENTS

1 tablespoon butter or olive oil

4 ears corn, kernels only

1 tablespoon fresh ginger root, peeled and minced

1 stalk lemongrass, bottom two-thirds smashed and chopped

4 garlic cloves, minced

2 tablespoons Thai red curry paste

4 tablespoons sriracha

4 cups (950ml/32fl oz) chicken broth

2 red-skinned potatoes, diced

1 15-ounce can coconut milk

¼ cup (7.5g/¼oz) Thai basil leaves, chopped

¼ cup (10g/⅓ oz) mint leaves, chopped

¼ cup (4g/⅛oz) cilantro leaves, chopped

Juice of 1 lime

2 tablespoons fish sauce

COOKING INSTRUCTIONS

1. Melt the butter or heat the olive oil in a large pot over medium heat.

2. Add the corn kernels, ginger, lemongrass, and garlic and sauté for 7 to 10 minutes, or until softened and fragrant.

3. Add the curry paste, sriracha, chicken broth, and potatoes. Increase the heat to high and bring to a boil. Reduce the heat to medium-low and simmer for 12 to 15 minutes, or until the potatoes are tender.

4. Add the coconut milk and stir to combine.

5. Transfer half of the mixture to a blender and puree for 30 seconds or until smooth. Pour the pureed soup back into the pot and stir to combine.

6. Stir in the basil, mint, cilantro, lime juice, and fish sauce and serve.

FIRE AND ICE GAZPACHO

Is it Spanish? Is it Mexican? Who cares! The only thing that really matters is that this soup, chilled yet full of tingly heat, is the right kinda refreshing when summer temps scorch.

INGREDIENTS

8 cups (1.2kg/45oz) seedless
   watermelon, chopped
   (about ¼ large melon)
2 large tomatoes, cored and roughly
   chopped
1 English cucumber, roughly chopped
4 basil sprigs, leaves only
4 cilantro sprigs, leaves only
4 mint sprigs, leaves only
3 tablespoons sriracha

1 teaspoon sea salt
2 tablespoons sherry vinegar
1 tablespoon olive oil

PICKLED ONIONS
1 tablespoon sugar
¼ cup (60ml/2fl oz) red wine vinegar
¼ cup (60ml/2fl oz) water
½ teaspoon mustard seeds
1 red onion, thinly sliced

COOKING INSTRUCTIONS

1. In a food processor or blender, process the watermelon in batches until smooth and no chunks remain. Transfer the watermelon juice to a large bowl.

2. In the same processor or blender, combine the tomatoes, cucumber, basil, cilantro, mint, sriracha, salt, and sherry vinegar. With the blade running, slowly pour in the olive oil and process until smooth. Transfer to the bowl with watermelon juice. Refrigerate until ready to serve. Note: This can be prepared a day ahead to give the flavors time to meld.

3. For the pickled red onions, combine the sugar, red wine vinegar, water, and mustard seeds in a small saucepan and heat just until the sugar melts. Pour the red onions into the pan, combine, and set aside. Note: This can be prepared a day or two ahead and stored in an airtight container in the refrigerator until ready to use.

4. Ladle soup into bowls and serve with the pickled onions.

SHRIMP TOM YUM SOUP

This is the one-pot dish to rule them all. Everything gets tossed in, simmered, strained, and then it's time to serve. While I won't say it's necessarily life-changing, it's damn near close.

INGREDIENTS

6 cups, or 1½ quarts (1.4l/48fl oz) chicken broth

4 tablespoons sriracha

4 kaffir lime leaves

1 (3-inch/8cm) piece fresh ginger root, unpeeled and mashed slightly with back of knife

1 (3-inch/8cm) slice lemongrass, mashed slightly with back of knife

4 button mushrooms, sliced

2 tablespoons soy sauce

2 tablespoons fish sauce

¼ cup (60ml/2fl oz) freshly squeezed lime juice (about 2 limes)

1 cup (150g/5¼oz) grape tomatoes, halved

¾ pound (340g) medium shrimp, peeled and deveined

2 scallions, chopped

COOKING INSTRUCTIONS

1. Bring the chicken broth to a boil in a large pot over high heat.

2. Add the sriracha, lime leaves, ginger root, and lemongrass. Reduce the heat to low and simmer for 15 minutes.

3. Strain the broth through a fine mesh strainer and discard the lime leaves, ginger root, and lemongrass. Return the stock to the pot over medium heat.

4. Add the mushrooms, soy sauce, fish sauce, lime juice, and tomatoes and simmer for 5 minutes.

5. Add the shrimp and scallions and cook for an additional 2 to 4 minutes, or until the shrimp are bright pink and no longer translucent. Serve immediately.

TRIPLE-THREAT CHILI

Unlike that crap boxed wine in your fridge, this'll get even better the next day. Prep it ahead of time, allowing the smoky, slightly sweet adobo pepper enough time to mingle and make friends.

INGREDIENTS

1 tablespoon olive oil

1 red bell pepper, seeded and diced

1 sweet onion, diced, divided

4 garlic cloves, minced

3 tablespoons sriracha

1 tablespoon ground cumin

1 tablespoon chili powder

1 teaspoon dried oregano

1 chipotle chile, chopped, plus
   1 tablespoon adobo sauce (from
   canned chipotles in adobo sauce)

1 pound (450g) lean ground beef

1 28-ounce can crushed tomatoes
   with juice

2 cups (475ml/16fl oz) beef broth

1 15-ounce can black beans, drained
   and rinsed

1 15-ounce can kidney beans, drained
   and rinsed

1 15-ounce can pinto beans, drained
   and rinsed

Sea salt, to taste

1½ cups (170g/6oz) extra-sharp cheddar,
   grated, for serving

1 cup (16g/½oz) cilantro, chopped,
   for serving

1 cup (235ml/8fl oz) sour cream,
   for serving

COOKING INSTRUCTIONS

1. Heat the olive oil in a large Dutch oven over medium heat.

2. Add the bell pepper and half of the onion and sauté, stirring occasionally, for 7 to 10 minutes, or until they begin to soften.

3. Add the garlic, sriracha, cumin, chili powder, oregano, chipotle chile, and adobo sauce. Stir constantly for 1 minute.

4. Increase the heat to high and add the ground beef. Cook, breaking up the meat and stirring constantly, for 3 to 5 minutes, or until the meat is no longer pink.

5. Add the crushed tomatoes and beef broth and bring to a boil. Reduce the heat, add the beans, and simmer, partially covered, for 45 minutes, stirring occasionally.

6. Taste the chili and season with salt as needed.

7. To serve, ladle the chili into bowls and top with cheddar, the remaining onion, cilantro, and sour cream.

SOUTHWESTERN TORTILLA SOUP

Leave those sodium-laden taco seasoning packets right where they belong—on the grocery store shelf. This homemade spice mix is as simple as it is fabulously earthy and warm and carries the soup.

INGREDIENTS

CHICKEN

3 boneless, skinless chicken breasts
   (about ¾ pound/12oz total)
1 tablespoon olive oil
1 tablespoon sriracha
1 teaspoon chili powder
1 teaspoon ground cumin
½ teaspoon sea salt

SOUP

2 tablespoons olive oil
½ sweet onion, diced
1 bell pepper, seeded and diced
1 cup (145g/5oz) corn kernels, fresh or
   frozen (½ pack frozen)
4 garlic cloves, minced
2 tablespoons tomato paste

2 tablespooons sriracha
1 teaspoon ground cumin
1 teaspoon chili powder
8 cups (1.9l/64fl oz) chicken broth
1 (15-ounce) can black beans, rinsed
   and drained
2 handfuls corn tortilla chips, for serving
1 avocado, diced, for serving
2 limes, quartered, for serving
½ cup (60g/2oz) queso fresco, crumbled,
   or Monterey jack cheese, shredded,
   for serving
¼ cup (4g/ ⅛ oz) cilantro leaves,
   chopped, for serving
¼ cup (60ml/2fl oz) sour cream or crema,
   for serving

COOKING INSTRUCTIONS

1. Preheat the oven to 400°F (200°C). Line a baking sheet with aluminum foil and set aside.

2. In a medium bowl, combine the chicken, olive oil, sriracha, chili powder, cumin, and salt. Mix well to coat. Arrange the chicken on the prepared baking sheet and bake for 15 to 20 minutes, or until cooked through. Remove from the oven and allow to cool for 10 minutes; when cool enough to handle, shred the chicken and set aside.

3. To prepare the soup, heat the olive oil in a large pot over medium-high heat.

4. Add the onion, bell pepper, corn, and garlic and sauté for 3 to 5 minutes, or until the onion and pepper begin to soften and caramelize.

Instructions continued on next page

SOUTHWESTERN TORTILLA SOUP

 Continue

COOKING INSTRUCTIONS

5. Add the tomato paste, sriracha, cumin, and chili powder and stir for 30 seconds, or until fragrant.

6. Add the chicken broth and beans and bring to a boil. Reduce the heat to low and simmer for 10 to 15 minutes.

7. Add the shredded chicken to the pot and adjust seasonings as needed.

8. To serve, ladle the soup into bowls and top with tortilla chips, diced avocado, lime wedges, queso fresco, cilantro, and sour cream.

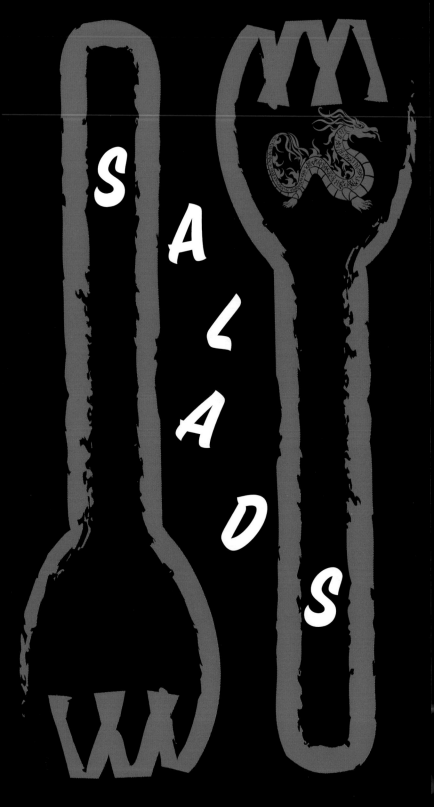

SALADS

KICKIN' BUFFALO CHICKEN SALAD

Serves 4

For the love of all things holy, stop buying bottled dressing! Instead of a gelatinous mix that forces you to fish for bleu cheese crumbles, dig into this plush blend that's chockablock with cheese.

INGREDIENTS

BLUE CHEESE DRESSING

½ cup (85g/3oz) blue cheese, crumbled

½ cup (120ml/4fl oz) good-quality mayonnaise

¼ cup (60ml/2fl oz) sour cream

2 tablespoons sriracha

1 teaspoon Worcestershire sauce

¼ teaspoon sea salt

½ teaspoon freshly ground black pepper

2 boneless, skinless chicken breasts, cut into ¾-inch (2cm) pieces

2 tablespoons all-purpose flour

1 teaspoon sea salt

1 teaspoon freshly ground black pepper

1 tablespoon olive oil

1 tablespoon unsalted butter

¼ cup (60ml/2fl oz) sriracha

1 teaspoon red wine vinegar

1 bunch or 10-ounce package baby spinach

3 carrots, shredded

4 celery stalks, chopped

COOKING INSTRUCTIONS

1. In a small bowl, prepare the blue cheese dressing. Combine the blue cheese, mayonnaise, sour cream, sriracha, Worcestershire, salt, and pepper and mix well. Set aside.

2. Combine the chicken with the flour, salt, and pepper in a large bowl and toss to coat.

3. Heat the olive oil and butter in a large nonstick skillet over medium-high heat until hot and bubbly.

4. Add the seasoned chicken pieces to the skillet and cook on the first side for 3 to 4 minutes. Turn the chicken and cook an additional 3 to 4 minutes, or until cooked through.

5. Stir in the sriracha and red wine vinegar and cook for 1 minute, stirring, until the chicken is coated.

6. On a large platter, arrange the baby spinach, carrots, and celery. Top with the hot chicken, drizzle on the blue cheese dressing, and serve.

DRAGON-STYLE MANGO SALAD

Serves

Sriracha and fish sauce combine to create one wicked umami bomb. But when swirled together with a citrusy brown sugar? You're looking at a one-step salad dressing that's nothing short of mind-blowing.

INGREDIENTS

¼ cup (20g/¾oz) shredded
   unsweetened coconut
2 unripe mangoes
2 cups (225g/8oz) bean sprouts
1 jalapeño, seeded and diced
½ cup (15g/½oz) Thai basil leaves
½ cup (8g/¼oz) cilantro leaves
4 scallions, green and white parts, cut
   into 2-inch (5cm) pieces
¼ cup (35g/1¼oz) roasted salted
   cashews, roughly chopped,
   for serving

CHILI DRESSING
¼ cup (60ml/2fl oz) fish sauce
¼ cup (60ml/2fl oz) freshly squeezed
   lime juice (about 2 limes)
2 tablespoons light brown sugar
2 tablespoons sriracha

COOKING INSTRUCTIONS

1. Place the coconut in a sauté pan over medium-low heat. Cook, stirring constantly, for about 2 to 3 minutes, or until lightly browned and fragrant. Transfer to a bowl to cool.

2. Peel the mangoes using a mandoline. Shred the peeled mango into long thin strips.

3. In a large bowl, combine the shredded mango, bean sprouts, diced jalapeño, basil, cilantro, and scallions.

4. In a small bowl, prepare the dressing. Whisk together the fish sauce, lime juice, brown sugar, and sriracha.

5. Pour the dressing over the mango salad and toss to coat.

6. Arrange on a serving platter and sprinkle with the toasted coconut and chopped cashews.

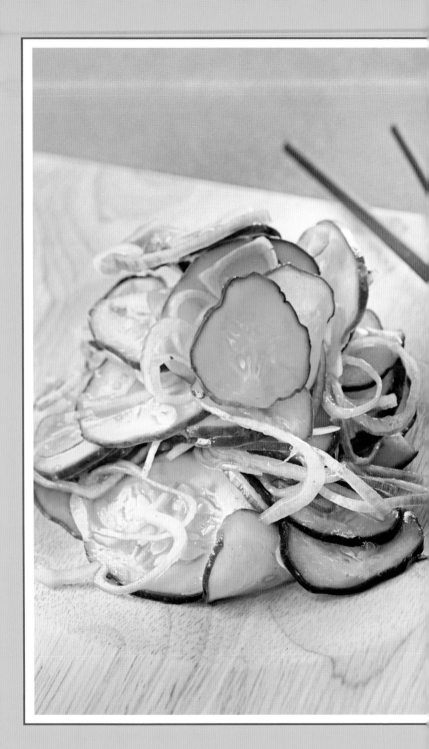

SPICY PICKLED-CUCUMBER SALAD

> **Serves 2 to 4**

It's about time this genteel Southern staple got some grit. When it comes to buying the cukes, don't get fancy. Kirbys are thin-skinned, making them the best for soaking up all that briny goodness.

INGREDIENTS

6 Kirby cucumbers

2 shallots

¼ cup (60ml/2fl oz) rice wine vinegar

2 tablespoons sriracha

2 tablespoons sugar

1 teaspoon sea salt

1 teaspoon sesame oil

COOKING INSTRUCTIONS

1. Using a mandoline or sharp knife, slice the cucumbers thinly and place in a large bowl. Repeat with the shallots, slicing as thinly as possible, and add them to the bowl.

2. In a medium bowl, whisk together the rice wine vinegar, sriracha, sugar, salt, and sesame oil. Pour the dressing over the cucumbers and shallots and toss to combine.

3. Transfer to an airtight container and allow to marinate for at least an hour or overnight, if possible. Great as an accompaniment with grilled sausages or meats.

CHILI CHICKPEA SALAD

Serves 4

Fair warning: Since this is a no-cook dish, there's nothing to diffuse the sweet heat of the sriracha. If you're feeling rushed for lunch, just slap some greens underneath this and serve with a heavy hand.

INGREDIENTS

1 tablespoon lemon zest (about 1 lemon)

¼ cup (60ml/2fl oz) freshly squeezed lemon juice (about 1½ lemons)

2 tablespoons sriracha

¼ cup (60ml/2fl oz) olive oil

½ teaspoon sea salt

½ teaspoon freshly ground black pepper

2 15-ounce cans chickpeas, drained and rinsed

1 cup (150g/5¼oz) grape tomatoes, halved

½ cup (85g/3oz) sheep's milk feta, crumbled

½ cup (30g/1oz) parsley leaves, roughly chopped

1½ celery stalks, thinly sliced

1 red onion, diced

COOKING INSTRUCTIONS

1. In a large bowl, whisk together the lemon zest, lemon juice, sriracha, olive oil, salt, and pepper.

2. Add the chickpeas, tomatoes, feta, parsley, celery, and red onion. Toss well with the dressing and allow to marinate for at least 30 minutes before serving.

BLACK AND BLUE CHICKEN-SPINACH SALAD

No one likes a procrastinator, so suck it up and prep this dish in steps: chop veggies the night before, marinate in the morning, and then whip up the sauce right before plating. Boom, dinner served.

INGREDIENTS

CHICKEN MARINADE

4 boneless, skinless chicken breasts

1 tablespoon olive oil

2 tablespoons sriracha

1 tablespoon lime zest (about 3 limes)

1 tablespoon freshly squeezed lime juice

1½ teaspoons ground cumin

1½ teaspoons chili powder

1 teaspoon sea salt

BLUE-CHEESE CHILI DRESSING

⅓ cup (80ml/2¾oz) mayonnaise

⅓ cup (80ml/2¾oz) sour cream

⅔ cup (100g/3½oz) blue cheese, crumbled

2 tablespoons 2% milk

2 tablespoons freshly squeezed lemon juice (about 1 lemon)

2 tablespoons sriracha

1 teaspoon Worcestershire sauce

½ teaspoon sea salt

½ teaspoon freshly ground black pepper

1 bunch or 10-ounce package baby spinach

1 cup (150g/5¼oz) cherry tomatoes, halved

2½ celery stalks, thinly sliced

2 carrots, peeled and thinly sliced

1 red onion, halved and thinly sliced

COOKING INSTRUCTIONS

1. To prepare the chicken, butterfly each breast horizontally so it lies flat, but do not cut all the way through.

2. In a large bowl, whisk together the olive oil, sriracha, lime zest, lime juice, cumin, chili powder, and salt. Add the butterflied chicken breasts and toss to coat. Cover and refrigerate at least 30 minutes or up to 2 hours. The longer it marinates, the more flavorful the grilled chicken will be.

Instructions continued on next page

BLACK AND BLUE CHICKEN-SPINACH SALAD

Continued

COOKING INSTRUCTIONS

3. Once the chicken is marinated, preheat a grill or grill pan over medium-high heat. Brush the grill or pan with olive oil or grease with olive oil spray.

4. Grill the chicken until marked and cooked through, turning once, about 4 to 6 minutes per side. Transfer to a cutting board and allow to rest for 10 minutes. Once rested, slice thinly and set aside.

5. While the chicken is resting, make the dressing. In a medium bowl, whisk together the mayonnaise, sour cream, blue cheese, milk, lemon juice, sriracha, Worcestershire, salt, and pepper.

6. To assemble the salad, layer the baby spinach, tomatoes, celery, carrots, red onion, and sliced chicken on a platter. Drizzle with the blue cheese dressing and serve.

APPETIZERS

SALTED HONEY-LIME POPCORN

Serves 4

Say hello to kettle corn's cousin. You know, the kind of cousin who lives abroad, smokes non-filters, and dates fabulously inappropriate people. Not quite sold? Repeat after me: Sriracha. Honey. Butter.

INGREDIENTS

1 tablespoon olive oil
½ cup (115g/4oz) popcorn kernels
2 tablespoons honey
2 tablespoons salted butter
2 tablespoons sriracha
1 tablespoon lime zest (about 3 limes)
½ to 1 tablespoon sea salt

COOKING INSTRUCTIONS

1. In a large pot with a tight-fitting lid, heat the olive oil over medium-high heat. Add the popcorn kernels and cover with lid.

2. While the popcorn is popping, heat the honey, butter, and sriracha in a small saucepan over medium-low heat until just melted. Remove from heat, stir in the lime zest, and cover to keep warm.

3. Once the popping begins to slow down, with about 5 seconds in between each pop, remove from heat.

4. Pour half of the popcorn into a large bowl, then drizzle with half of the sriracha-honey butter and sprinkle in half of the salt. Repeat with the remaining popcorn, sriracha honey butter, and salt. Stir well and serve immediately.

CRACKLIN' CANDIED BACON

Serves

Something magical happens when you rub bacon down with spicy sugar and pop it in the oven. Unlike the flabby stovetop stuff, this method gives you crackling, swoon-worthy strips of sweet-salty perfection.

INGREDIENTS

2 tablespoons sriracha

¾ cup (165g/6oz) firmly packed light brown sugar

1 pound (450g) thickly cut slices smoked bacon (about 12 slices)

COOKING INSTRUCTIONS

1. Preheat the oven to 300°F (150°C). Line a large baking sheet with parchment paper and set aside.

2. Combine the sriracha and brown sugar in a small bowl.

3. Coat each slice of bacon in the sugar mixture, rubbing both sides to ensure that the mixture adheres to the bacon.

4. Arrange the bacon strips on the prepared baking sheet so they are close together but not overlapping. Bake for 30 minutes without turning.

5. Allow to cool completely on the baking sheet, then break apart and serve.

GRILLED CHEESE EN FUEGO

Serves 2

This grilled cheese gets decidedly adult. Nutty gruyère and biting sourdough do their part, but the secret is the Honeycrisp apples—sweet, snappy, and totally worth the cost. Don't even give Red Delicious a second thought.

INGREDIENTS

¼ cup (60g/2oz) salted butter, at room temperature (½ stick)

4 slices sourdough or other favorite great-quality bread

4 tablespoons sriracha

1 cup (115g/4oz) gruyère cheese, grated

½ cup Honeycrisp or other favorite apple, cored and thinly sliced (about ⅓ apple)

COOKING INSTRUCTIONS

1. Heat a medium frying pan over medium-low heat.

2. Spread 1 tablespoon butter on the outside of each slice of bread.

3. Spread 1 tablespoon sriracha on the inside of each slice of bread.

4. On two of the sriracha-smothered sides, sprinkle the gruyère and arrange the apple slices. Close the sandwiches with the remaining slices of bread, sriracha side down.

5. Once the frying pan is warm, add the sandwiches and fry until the bread is browned and the cheese is melted, about 3 to 5 minutes. Flip and fry for another 3 to 5 minutes. Serve immediately.

FIERY GLAZED NUTS

Serves

This recipe is the lazy cook's secret weapon. Take it to parties, pack it up for presents, or stuff it straight down your gullet. Just don't underestimate its stealthy delivery system for addictive deliciousness.

INGREDIENTS

Cooking spray

¼ cup (60ml/2fl oz) honey

2 tablespoons sriracha

1 tablespoon salted butter, melted

1 teaspoon kosher salt

1 cup (100g/3½oz) raw walnut halves

1 cup (100g/3½oz) raw or untoasted pecans

1 cup (145g/5oz) raw almonds

1 cup (140g/5oz) raw cashews

COOKING INSTRUCTIONS

1. Preheat the oven to 300°F (150°C). Line a large baking sheet with aluminum foil and spray with cooking spray. Set aside.

2. In a large bowl, combine the honey, sriracha, melted butter, and salt. Add the nuts and stir to coat well.

3. Spread the coated nuts in a single layer on the prepared baking sheet. Bake for 10 minutes, stir the nuts, then return to the oven. Repeat three to four times for a total of 40 to 50 minutes in the oven. Watch the nuts carefully; you want them to be golden brown. They can burn very quickly.

4. Remove from the oven and allow to cool completely. Transfer to an airtight container to store for up to one week.

SMOKIN' SWEET CORN SALSA

Serves 8

If you're still finding your footing in the kitchen, make friends with this salsa. Broiling the corn till it's nice and smoky gives it an upscale feel, but beyond that, all you're doing is chopping and mixing.

INGREDIENTS

2 ears sweet corn, shucked

2 tomatoes, quartered

1 sweet onion, peeled and quartered

1 jalapeño, stemmed and cut in half

2 tablespoons sriracha

1 tablespoon olive oil

1 cup (285g/10oz) canned black-eyed peas, drained and rinsed

¼ cup (4g/⅛oz) cilantro, chopped

1 tablespoon red wine vinegar

1 teaspoon sea salt

Tortilla chips (optional)

COOKING INSTRUCTIONS

1. Heat the broiler. Line a baking sheet with aluminum foil and set aside.

2. In a large bowl, combine the corncobs, tomatoes, onion, jalapeño, sriracha, and olive oil. Toss well to coat. Transfer the mixture to the prepared baking sheet and broil for 8 to 10 minutes, stirring every 2 minutes, until charred. Allow to cool for 10 minutes.

3. To prepare the salsa, cut the corn kernels off the cobs and into a large bowl. Roughly chop the tomatoes, onion, and jalapeño and add to the corn.

4. Add the black-eyed peas, cilantro, red wine vinegar, and salt and toss to combine. Serve with tortilla chips or as a topping for your favorite tacos.

DEVILISH EGGS

Ensure these crazy-good eggs stay that way by using a non-reactive bowl during prep. In normal-people speak, this means stainless steel, ceramic, glass, or enamel—unless you like eggs that taste like metal.

INGREDIENTS

12 large hard-boiled eggs
½ cup (120ml/4fl oz) mayonnaise
¼ cup (60ml/2fl oz) sriracha
2 tablespoons milk
2 tablespoons Dijon mustard
2 teaspoons fresh cilantro, chopped
1 teaspoon sea salt
2 teaspoons smoked paprika

COOKING INSTRUCTIONS

1. Allow the boiled eggs to cool until you can handle them. Peel and slice the eggs in half lengthwise. Remove the yolks and place in a large non-reactive bowl. Set the whites aside and cover with a damp paper towel to keep them from drying out.

2. To the egg yolks, add the mayonnaise, sriracha, milk, Dijon, cilantro, and salt. Using a handheld mixer for a smooth texture or a wooden spoon for a chunkier texture, mix until well combined and smooth.

3. Spoon or pipe the yolk mixture into the reserved egg whites and sprinkle with paprika.

4. If not serving immediately, cover tightly with plastic wrap and refrigerate.

CRISPY CAULIFLOWER HOT "WINGS"

No offense to Frank and his hot sauce, but this version is the balls. Tip: If you don't have buttermilk for the dip, add 1 tablespoon of lemon juice to 1 cup (235ml/8fl oz) of milk and measure accordingly.

INGREDIENTS

4 cups, or 1 quart (950ml/32fl oz) canola oil
1½ cups (240g/8½oz) brown rice flour
1½ cups (355ml/12fl oz) whole milk
1 tablespoon garlic powder
1 tablespoon sea salt
¾ cup (175ml/6fl oz) sriracha
½ cup (115g/4oz) salted butter, melted
   (1 stick)
1 head cauliflower, trimmed and cut into
   bite-size pieces

BLUE CHEESE DIP
¾ cup (115g/4oz) gorgonzola, crumbled
⅓ cup (80ml/2¾fl oz) sour cream
⅓ cup (80ml/2¾fl oz) buttermilk
¼ cup (60ml/2fl oz) mayonnaise
¼ cup (60ml/2fl oz) sriracha
1 tablespoon apple cider vinegar
1 teaspoon Worcestershire sauce
½ teaspoon freshly ground black pepper

COOKING INSTRUCTIONS

1. Heat the canola oil in a large pot over medium-high heat until the oil reaches 350°F (180°C).

2. While the oil heats, make the cauliflower batter. In a large bowl, combine the brown rice flour, milk, garlic powder, and salt and mix until well combined.

3. In another large bowl, whisk together the sriracha and melted butter and set aside.

4. Once the oil is hot, fry the cauliflower. Working in batches, dip the cauliflower pieces into the prepared batter to coat completely, then carefully drop them into the oil. Do not overcrowd the pot. Fry the cauliflower for 2 to 3 minutes, or until golden brown. Flip and fry for another 2 to 3 minutes. Continue with remaining cauliflower.

5. Again working in batches, transfer the crispy browned cauliflower to the sriracha mixture and toss to coat. Place sriracha-coated cauliflower on a large plate or platter and continue with remaining fried cauliflower.

6. To make the blue cheese dip, combine the gorgonzola, sour cream, buttermilk, mayonnaise, sriracha, apple cider vinegar, Worcestershire sauce, and pepper in a medium bowl and mix well.

7. Serve the crispy, coated cauliflower bites with the blue cheese dip on the side.

BLACK BEAN HUMMUS WITH FIVE-SPICE PITA CHIPS

Store-bought chips are for suckers. By cutting up fresh pitas and toasting them yourself, you'll be rewarded with a super-sturdy chip that's golden brown, crisp, and perfectly flavored with this surefire spice mix.

INGREDIENTS

SRIRACHA PITA CHIPS
2 tablespoons olive oil
2 tablespoons sriracha
1½ teaspoons ground cumin
½ teaspoon chili powder
½ teaspoon cayenne pepper
½ teaspoon garlic powder
½ teaspoon sea salt
4 pita breads, cut into 8 wedges each

HUMMUS
1 15-ounce can black beans, drained and rinsed
¼ cup (60ml/2fl oz) sriracha
¼ cup (60ml/2fl oz) tahini paste
¼ cup (60ml/2fl oz) freshly squeezed lemon juice (about 1½ lemons)
2 garlic cloves
1½ teaspoons ground cumin
¼ teaspoon cayenne pepper
1 teaspoon sea salt
2 tablespoons olive oil

COOKING INSTRUCTIONS

1. Preheat the oven to 375°F (190°C). Line two large baking sheets with parchment paper and set aside.

2. In a large bowl, combine the olive oil, sriracha, cumin, chili powder, cayenne, garlic powder, and salt and mix well to combine. Add the pita wedges and toss to coat.

3. Arrange the pita wedges in a single layer on the prepared baking sheets. Bake for 7 to 8 minutes. Toss the pitas and turn the baking sheets, then return to the oven for an additional 7 to 8 minutes, or until browned and crispy. Let cool completely before serving. Note: The pita chips may be prepared ahead of time and stored in an airtight container for up to three days.

4. To make the hummus, combine the black beans, sriracha, tahini, lemon juice, garlic, cumin, cayenne, and salt in a food processor. Process for about 2 minutes, or until smooth. With the motor running, slowly pour in the olive oil and process for 30 seconds to 1 minute longer, or until smooth and the oil is well incorporated.

5. Serve the hummus with the cooled pita chips.

CHEESY JALAPEÑO POPPERS WITH ZESTY RANCH

Makes 16 poppers

OK, I'm not going to lie. These guys aren't quick. But they're creamy, crunchy, and bubbling over with cheese—in other words, totally worth it. Plus, let's talk sauce: two ingredients, one step...genius.

INGREDIENTS

¾ cup (170g/6oz) cream cheese, at room temperature

1½ cups (170g/6oz) extra-sharp cheddar cheese, grated

2 tablespoons sriracha

1 pound (450g) jalapeño peppers (about 16 peppers), halved through the stem and seeded

½ cup (120ml/4fl oz) milk

½ cup (60g/2oz) all-purpose flour

½ cup (55g/2oz) plain breadcrumbs

3 cups (710ml/24fl oz) vegetable or canola oil

ZESTY RANCH DIP

1 cup (235ml/8fl oz) favorite ranch dressing

¼ cup (60ml/2fl oz) sriracha

COOKING INSTRUCTIONS

1. In a medium bowl, mix the softened cream cheese, grated cheddar cheese, and sriracha until smooth and well blended. Spoon this mixture into the jalapeño halves; using the cheese mixture as "glue," stick the halves back together to form whole jalapeños. Set aside.

2. Pour the milk, flour, and breadcrumbs into three separate bowls.

3. Dip the jalapeños in the milk and then in the flour to coat completely, working in batches if necessary. Transfer the flour-coated jalapeños to a plate or baking sheet that fits in your freezer. Freeze the jalapeños for 10 minutes. Reserve the milk and discard the flour.

4. Dip the frozen jalapeños in the milk again and then roll them in the breadcrumbs, making sure they are fully coated. Transfer back to the plate or baking sheet and return them to the freezer for another 10 minutes.

5. While the jalapeños freeze, heat the vegetable or canola oil in a large, deep skillet until the oil reaches 365°F (185°C).

Instructions continued on next page

CHEESY JALAPEÑO POPPERS WITH ZESTY RANCH

Continu

COOKING INSTRUCTIONS

6. Preheat the oven to 350°F (180°C). Fit a baking sheet with a wire rack and set aside.

7. Deep-fry the coated jalapeños in batches for 2 to 3 minutes per batch, or until golden brown. Transfer the fried jalapeños to a paper towel–lined plate and let drain. Continue frying the remaining jalapeños and set them aside to drain.

8. Once drained, transfer to the prepared wire rack. Bake for 5 to 7 minutes, or until the jalapeños have softened and the cheese is oozing out.

9. While the jalapeños bake, make the dip. In a small bowl, whisk together the ranch dressing and sriracha.

10. Serve the hot jalapeño poppers with the sriracha-ranch dip.

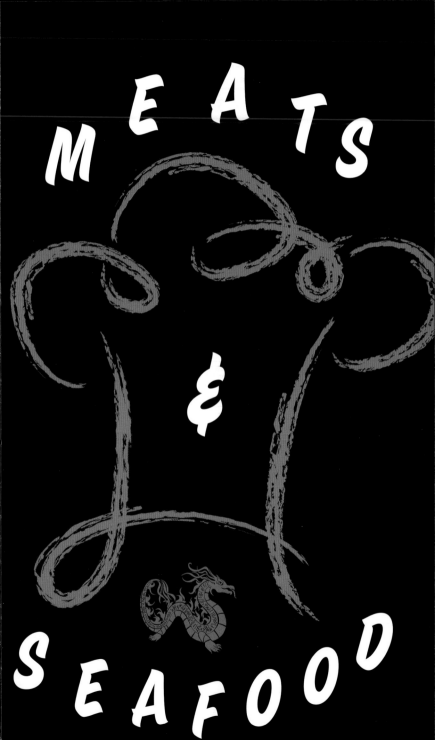

MEATS
&
SEAFOOD

LEMONGRASS-SKEWERED CHILI-GLAZED SHRIMP

Makes 8 ske[wers]

No cookout would be complete without a little competition. Show up the a-hole who brought the bland pre-made burgers with this zippy dish that'd give your local Thai restaurant a run for its money.

INGREDIENTS

SHRIMP MARINADE

1 pound (450g) extra-large shrimp (about 24 shrimp), peeled and deveined

4 tablespoons fish sauce

2 tablespoons sriracha

2 tablespoons honey

1 tablespoon sesame oil

1 tablespoon ginger root, peeled and minced or grated

2 garlic cloves, minced

Zest of 1 lime (juice reserved for the sauce)

DIPPING SAUCE

2 tablespoons sriracha

1 tablespoon honey

1 lemongrass stalk, white part bruised and finely chopped

1 garlic clove, minced

1 teaspoon fresh ginger root, peeled and finely grated

Juice of 1 lime

1 scallion, finely chopped

2 lemongrass stalks

COOKING INSTRUCTIONS

1. Combine the shrimp, fish sauce, sriracha, honey, sesame oil, ginger, garlic, and lime zest in a medium bowl and mix well. Cover and allow to marinate for at least 2 to 3 hours or overnight.

2. In a medium bowl, prepare the dipping sauce. Combine the sriracha, honey, chopped lemongrass, garlic, ginger, lime juice and chopped scallion in a medium bowl and mix well. Allow to sit until ready to serve.

3. To cook the shrimp, preheat a grill or grill pan to medium-high heat.

4. To prepare the lemongrass skewers, trim the tops and root ends of the stalks, then carefully peel off the outer layer. Cut the stalks into four 6-inch (15cm) skewers, then cut each in half lengthwise for eight skewers total. Cut one end of the skewers on the diagonal so you have a pointed end for skewering the shrimp.

5. Skewer three shrimp onto each lemongrass stalk. Transfer the skewers to the preheated grill or pan and grill 2 to 3 minutes per side, until the shrimp are slightly charred and pink throughout.

6. Serve the grilled shrimp skewers with the dipping sauce.

SRIRACHA PULLED-PORK TACOS WITH PICKLED ONIONS

Makes 16 tacos

If you think slow cookers are just for moms, well, get over yourself—unless you're one of those hipster types who eschews fuss-free cooking with guaranteed results. In that case, just stop reading.

INGREDIENTS

SPICE RUB
¼ cup (60ml/2fl oz) sriracha
¼ cup (30g/1oz) chili powder
1 tablespoon kosher salt
1 tablespoon light brown sugar
2 teaspoons ground cumin
1 teaspoon cayenne pepper
1 teaspoon Mexican dried oregano
1 teaspoon onion powder
1 teaspoon garlic powder
½ teaspoon ground cinnamon
⅛ teaspoon ground cloves

3½ pounds (1.6kg/56oz) boneless pork
    shoulder roast
2 tablespoons olive oil
16 corn tortillas, warmed, for serving
1 cup (16g/½oz) cilantro leaves, for
    serving
1 recipe Pickled Onions (see page 25),
    for serving
2 limes, quartered, for serving
1 avocado, peeled and diced, for serving

COOKING INSTRUCTIONS

1. To make the spice rub, combine the sriracha, chili powder, salt, brown sugar, cumin, cayenne, oregano, onion powder, garlic powder, cinnamon, and cloves in a small bowl and mix well.

2. Rub the pork roast with the spice rub and marinate in a covered bowl in the refrigerator overnight.

3. To cook the pork, heat the olive oil in a large frying pan over medium-high heat. Add the marinated roast and sear until brown on all sides, about 12 minutes total.

4. Place the seared roast in a slow cooker. Cook on low for 6 to 8 hours, until the pork is falling apart and tender. If you don't have a slow cooker, transfer the roast to a Dutch oven and cook at 300°F (150°C) for 4 hours.

5. Transfer the roast to a cutting board. Allow the juices in the slow cooker or Dutch oven to cool, then skim off all the fat, leaving only the juices.

6. Cut the roast into large chunks. Using two forks, shred the meat. Return the shredded meat to the slow cooker and toss to coat with the roast juices.

7. To serve, pile the pulled pork onto warmed corn tortillas and garnish with cilantro, pickled onions, limes, and avocado.

FIREHOUSE BEEF SLIDERS

Makes 12 slid...

"Mmm, this is one amazingly dry, crumbly burger," said no one ever. To achieve that juicy drip-down-your-chin experience, remember this: fat is your friend. Always opt for beef with an 80/20 ratio of lean meat to fat.

INGREDIENTS

2 pounds (900g) premium ground beef (80% lean/20% fat)

3 tablespoons sriracha

1 tablespoon Dijon mustard

2 tablespoons olive oil, plus more for grilling

3 garlic cloves, minced

1 teaspoon sea salt

1 teaspoon freshly ground black pepper

1½ cups (170g/6oz) extra-sharp cheddar cheese, grated

12 small brioche buns, sliced in half

½ cup (120ml/4fl oz) ketchup

¼ cup (60ml/2fl oz) sriracha

1 head butter lettuce

2 red onions, thinly sliced into rounds

COOKING INSTRUCTIONS

1. Heat a grill or grill pan to medium-high heat.

2. In a large bowl, combine the ground beef, sriracha, Dijon, olive oil, garlic, salt, and pepper. Mix gently and shape into twelve 2-inch (5cm) patties of equal size and thickness.

3. When the grill is hot, brush the grill grate or pan with olive oil. Grill the burgers for 4 minutes. Flip with a spatula and grill another 4 to 6 minutes for medium-rare, or longer if you prefer more well-done. For the last 2 minutes of grilling time, place 2 tablespoons cheddar on top of each burger and close the grill lid. Transfer the sliders to a platter and tent with aluminum foil to keep warm.

4. Toast the buns on the grill or pan, cut side down, for about 1 minute.

5. Whisk together the ketchup and sriracha in a small bowl.

6. To assemble the sliders, divide the butter lettuce among the twelve bottom buns. Top each with a burger, then finish with sriracha ketchup and red onion. Cover burgers with the top buns and serve hot.

"CIN" CITY SPAGHETTI

If you're from Cincinnati, you'll call this dish a "5-Way." If you're from anywhere else, you'll just call it one friggin' delicious pile of 'sketti. Do like the locals and layer that sucker high with grated cheese.

INGREDIENTS

2 tablespoons olive oil

2 pounds (900g) lean ground beef

2 small sweet onions, one diced and the other minced

2 garlic cloves, minced

1 teaspoon sea salt

1 teaspoon freshly ground black pepper

¼ cup (30g/1oz) chili powder

¼ cup (60ml/2fl oz) sriracha

1 teaspoon unsweetened cocoa powder

2 teaspoons ground cumin

1 teaspoon ground cinnamon

½ teaspoon ground allspice

½ teaspoon cayenne pepper

1 28-ounce can crushed tomatoes with juice

½ cup (120ml/4fl oz) beef broth

1 bay leaf

2 tablespoons Worcestershire sauce

2 tablespoons sherry vinegar

1 15-ounce can kidney beans, drained and rinsed

1 pound (450g) spaghetti, cooked according to package directions

3 cups (340g/12oz) extra-sharp cheddar cheese, grated, for serving

COOKING INSTRUCTIONS

1. Heat the olive oil in a large pot or Dutch oven over medium heat.

2. Add the ground beef, diced onion, and garlic. Season with salt and pepper and cook, stirring and breaking up the meat, for 5 to 7 minutes, or until the meat is browned.

3. Add the chili powder, sriracha, cocoa powder, cumin, cinnamon, allspice, and cayenne. Cook for 2 to 3 minutes, stirring frequently.

4. Add the crushed tomatoes, beef broth, bay leaf, Worcestershire, and sherry vinegar. Bring to a simmer and cook for 1 hour, stirring often.

5. Add the kidney beans, then taste and adjust seasonings accordingly. Discard the bay leaf.

6. To serve, spoon the chili over the spaghetti and top with the minced onion and cheddar.

GINGERED CRAB WITH TOASTED COCONUT

Thai bird chili is a dried chili that's fierce and unique in flavor. It's worth tracking one down for this, but if you can't (ahem, lazy), try swapping in a serrano chili or even crushed red pepper flakes.

INGREDIENTS

1 pound (450g) king crab legs, broken into pieces
¼ cup (60ml/2fl oz) tomato paste
¼ cup (60ml/2fl oz) sriracha
2 tablespoons oyster sauce
2 tablespoons dark soy sauce
1 tablespoon dark brown sugar
¼ cup (60ml/2fl oz) water
¼ cup (60ml/2fl oz) peanut oil

4 scallions, thinly sliced
1 tablespoon fresh ginger root, peeled and minced
4 garlic cloves, minced
1 Thai bird chili, minced
¼ cup (4g/⅛oz) cilantro leaves
¼ cup (20g/⅛oz) shredded unsweetened coconut, toasted

COOKING INSTRUCTIONS

1. Slightly crack the pieces of crab legs. Set aside.

2. In a medium bowl, combine the tomato paste, sriracha, oyster sauce, soy sauce, brown sugar, and water. Mix well and set aside.

3. Heat a large wok over high heat and add the peanut oil. Add the scallions, ginger, garlic, and chili and cook for 1 minute, stirring constantly.

4. Add the crab legs and cook for 1 minute longer.

5. Add the sriracha-tomato sauce and cook for another 5 minutes, or until the crab has absorbed the sauce and it has begun to thicken.

6. Arrange the crab legs on a platter and garnish with the cilantro and toasted coconut. Serve immediately.

SPICY FRIED OYSTER PO' BOY

Serves 4

After an epic night, a next-day shower is the only way to feel human again, no?
Same principle applies to oysters. A soothing milk bath bounces them back to life
and makes them taste fresh.

INGREDIENTS

3 dozen oysters, shucked and liquid
    reserved

1 cup (235ml/8fl oz) whole milk

2 large eggs

¼ cup (60ml/2fl oz) sriracha

1 cup (125g/4½oz) all-purpose flour

½ cup (60g/2oz) yellow cornmeal

2 teaspoons Cajun seasoning

1 teaspoon sea salt

3 cups (710ml/24fl oz) vegetable oil

4 French baguettes, 6 inches (15cm)
    each, halved lengthwise

4 cups (85g/3oz) mixed baby greens

2 large tomatoes, thinly sliced

SRIRACHA MAYONNAISE

1 cup (235ml/8fl oz) good-quality
    mayonnaise

½ cup (120ml/4fl oz) sriracha

1 tablespoon Cajun seasoning

COOKING INSTRUCTIONS

1.   Combine the oysters and milk in a medium bowl and let stand for 20 minutes.

2.   In another medium bowl, whisk together the eggs, 1 tablespoon reserved oyster
     liquid, and sriracha.

3.   In a third medium bowl, whisk together the flour, cornmeal, Cajun seasoning,
     and salt.

4.   Heat the vegetable oil in a large Dutch oven over medium-high heat until the oil
     reaches 360°F (180°C).

5.   Drain the oysters from the milk and dredge in the egg mixture. Drip off excess
     egg mixture, then dredge the oysters in the flour mixture, making sure to coat
     completely.

6.   Working in batches, fry the oysters for 3 to 4 minutes, or until golden brown.
     Drain on paper towels.

7.   While the oysters are frying, prepare the sriracha mayonnaise. In a medium
     bowl, whisk together the mayonnaise, sriracha, and Cajun seasoning. Set aside.

8.   To assemble the sandwiches, open the sliced baguettes, then layer the baby
     greens, tomato slices, and fried oysters on the bottom halves. Drizzle the
     sriracha mayonnaise on top. Top with the remaining baguette halves and serve
     immediately.

CHILI-GLAZED BABY BACK RIBS

Serves 6

Cilantro leaves are the only green we'll allow near our ribs. You'd be surprised how they perk up the glossy, glazed, piggy goodness. If you hate it, skip it. We'll only judge a little.

INGREDIENTS

5 pounds (2.3kg) baby back pork ribs, silver skin removed (about 2 racks)

Olive oil, for grilling

2 teaspoons kosher salt

½ cup (120ml/4fl oz) sweet soy sauce

½ cup (120ml/4fl oz) sriracha

¼ cup (60ml/2fl oz) root beer

½ cup (8g/¼oz) cilantro leaves

COOKING INSTRUCTIONS

1. Allow the ribs to reach room temperature, about 30 minutes to 1 hour.

2. Heat a grill and prepare for indirect grilling at 300°F (150°C). Lightly oil the grill.

3. Sprinkle the salt over the meat side of the ribs. Arrange the ribs, bone side down, over the coolest part of the grill. Close the lid and grill for 2 hours. To test for doneness, insert a knife into the rib meat: if it slides out easily, the ribs are done.

4. Line a large rimmed baking sheet with aluminum foil. Transfer the grilled ribs to the prepared baking sheet.

5. Increase the grill temperature to 350°F (180°C).

6. Combine the soy sauce, sriracha, and root beer in a medium bowl and mix well. Set aside ½ cup (120ml/4fl oz) of this sauce for dipping.

7. Brush the top of the ribs with half of the remaining sauce. Transfer the ribs to the grill, still over indirect heat, sauced side down. Grill for 10 minutes.

8. Brush the other side of the ribs with the remaining sauce. Flip over and grill for another 10 minutes.

9. Transfer the ribs back to the baking sheet and allow to rest for 10 minutes, lightly covered. Cut into the ribs and serve with the remaining sauce drizzled over and cilantro scattered on top.

SHORTCUT CAJUN JAMBALAYA

Authentic Cajun soul food that doesn't require hours of practice, cook time, or listening to someone's rambling grandmother? Sign us up. If you're feelin' fancy, swap in some lobster for that crawfish.

INGREDIENTS

2 tablespoons unsalted butter

2 tablespoons olive oil

1 onion, chopped

3 celery stalks, chopped

6 garlic cloves, minced

2 boneless, skinless chicken breasts,
    cut into ½-inch (1.5cm) cubes

½ pound (225g) spicy Andouille sausage,
    cut into ½-inch (1.5cm) cubes

3 bay leaves

1½ teaspoons dried thyme

1 teaspoon smoked paprika

2½ cups (460g/16oz) uncooked long-grain
    white rice

1 28-ounce can stewed tomatoes
    with juice

1 cup (235ml/8fl oz) chicken broth

¼ cup (60ml/2fl oz) sriracha

¼ cup (60ml/2fl oz) Worcestershire sauce

1½ teaspoons sea salt

1 pound (450g) medium shrimp, peeled
    and deveined

1 pound (450g) crawfish meat

¼ cup (15g/½oz) fresh parsley, chopped

COOKING INSTRUCTIONS

1. Heat the butter and olive oil in a large, deep skillet over medium-high heat until hot and bubbly.

2. Add the onion, celery, and garlic and cook, stirring occasionally, for about 5 minutes, or until the vegetables begin to lightly brown and soften.

3. Add the chicken and Andouille sausage and cook, stirring frequently, for about 5 minutes, or until the chicken is no longer pink.

4. Add the bay leaves, thyme, paprika, and rice and cook for 1 minute, stirring constantly.

5. Stir in the stewed tomatoes with their juice, chicken broth, sriracha, Worcestershire, and salt. Bring to a boil, then reduce heat to a simmer and cook for about 30 minutes, covered, until the rice is tender.

6. Remove the lid and add the shrimp and crawfish. Stir until the shrimp and crawfish are just cooked through, about 3 minutes.

7. Scatter over the parsley and serve.

HELLFIRE TUNA BURGERS

Serves

There's plenty of fish in the sea, but here's the catch: not all are created equal. Buy sushi-grade tuna from a trusted fishmonger, making sure it's clearly marked and handled separately from all other fish.

INGREDIENTS

2 pounds (900g) sushi-grade ahi tuna, diced

1 jalapeño, seeded and minced

¼ cup (60ml/2fl oz) sriracha

3 tablespoons soy sauce

2 tablespoons good-quality mayonnaise

7 scallions, green and white parts, minced

2 tablespoons toasted sesame seeds

1 tablespoon fresh ginger root, peeled and minced

¼ cup (28g/1oz) panko (Japanese breadcrumbs)

2 tablespoons sesame oil

4 pineapple rounds, ¼-inch (0.5cm) thick

4 brioche buns, split in half

4 butter lettuce leaves (about ⅓ head)

SRIRACHA-HOISIN SAUCE

¼ cup (60ml/2fl oz) hoisin sauce

¼ cup (60ml/2fl oz) sriracha

COOKING INSTRUCTIONS

1. Preheat a griddle or large sauté pan over high heat.

2. In a large bowl, combine the diced tuna, jalapeño, sriracha, soy sauce, mayonnaise, scallions, sesame seeds, ginger, and panko until just mixed. Form into four patties.

3. Brush the hot griddle or pan with sesame oil. Sear the burgers for 2 minutes per side for medium-rare or longer for more well-done burgers. Transfer to a plate and tent with aluminum foil to keep warm.

4. On the same griddle, sear the pineapple rounds for 1 minute per side.

5. In a small bowl, prepare the sauce. Whisk together the hoisin and sriracha.

6. To assemble the burgers, spread one-quarter of the sriracha-hoisin sauce on each bottom bun. Layer with lettuce, tuna burger, pineapple round, and top bun. Serve hot.

VIETNAMESE BANH MI WITH CHILI MAYO

Having a Napoleon complex is a great way to lose friends and alienate people—except in the case of these wee meatballs. Their big, brassy personality and over-achieving flavor will win over any room.

INGREDIENTS

CHILI MAYONNAISE

⅔ cup (160ml/5½fl oz) good-quality mayonnaise

⅓ cup (80ml/2¾fl oz) sriracha

1 tablespoon cilantro, chopped

1 scallion, chopped

MEATBALLS

1 pound (450g) ground pork

¼ cup (7.5g/¼oz) Thai basil, chopped

4 garlic cloves, minced

2 scallions, chopped

2 tablespoons sriracha

2 tablespoons fish sauce

2 teaspoons cornstarch

2 teaspoons light brown sugar

1 teaspoon kosher salt

PICKLED CARROTS

6 large carrots, coarsely grated

¼ cup (60ml/2fl oz) unsweetened rice vinegar

¼ cup (50g/1¾oz) sugar

1 teaspoon kosher salt

1 teaspoon toasted sesame oil

4 mini baguettes, about 8 to 10 inches (20 to 25cm) each

2 jalapeños, thinly sliced

2 cups (30g/1oz) cilantro leaves

COOKING INSTRUCTIONS

1. To make the chili mayonnaise, mix together the mayonnaise, sriracha, cilantro, and scallion in a small bowl. Cover and refrigerate until ready to use.

2. To make the meatballs, preheat the oven to 400°F (200°C). Line a rimmed baking sheet with aluminum foil and fit with a wire rack.

3. In a large bowl, gently mix the pork, basil, garlic, scallions, sriracha, fish sauce, cornstarch, brown sugar, and salt.

4. Using wet hands, form the pork mixture into 1-tablespoon meatballs and transfer to the wire rack. Bake for 15 minutes, or until browned and cooked through.

Instructions continued on next page

VIETNAMESE BANH MI
WITH CHILI MAYO

Continu

COOKING INSTRUCTIONS

5. While the meatballs are cooking, prepare the pickled carrots. Combine the carrots, rice vinegar, sugar, salt, and sesame oil in a large bowl and toss to coat. Allow to sit while you make the sandwiches.

6. Slice each baguette in half lengthwise. Remove enough bread from the center of each half to form a shell.

7. Spread the chili mayo over each baguette shell, then top with the sliced jalapeños, cilantro, and pickled carrots. Fill each sandwich with one-quarter of the meatballs and press the top baguette half over the filling to close the sandwich. Serve immediately.

VEGETABLES & SIDES

TWICE-BAKED CHILI POTATOES

Serves 6

Nobody puts potatoes in a corner. These dreamy, over-the-top taters are as seductive as Swayze, proving that the humble tuber deserves all the stage—erm, table—time it can get.

INGREDIENTS

3 russet potatoes

3 sweet potatoes

¾ cup (85g/3oz) extra-sharp cheddar cheese, grated

⅔ cup (160ml/5½fl oz) sour cream

¼ cup (60g/2oz) salted butter (½ stick)

⅓ cup (80ml/2¾fl oz) milk

¼ cup (60ml/2fl oz) sriracha

¼ cup (12g/½oz) chives, minced

1 teaspoon salt

1 teaspoon freshly ground black pepper

COOKING INSTRUCTIONS

1. Preheat the oven to 400°F (200°C). Line a baking sheet with aluminum foil and set aside.

2. Wash and pierce the russet and sweet potatoes with a fork or knife. Set on the prepared baking sheet and bake for 60 to 70 minutes, or until a knife inserted in the center comes out easily. Allow to cool for 10 minutes.

3. Cut each russet potato in half lengthwise. Scoop out the flesh from each half of potato, leaving the skin intact. Place the flesh in a large bowl.

4. Scoop out the flesh from the sweet potatoes, discarding the skin, and add to the bowl of russet potato flesh.

5. Add the cheddar, sour cream, butter, milk, sriracha, chives, salt, and pepper to the bowl. Using a handheld mixer, blend until smooth and creamy.

6. Stuff the mixture into each half of russet potato skin and place back on the baking sheet.

7. Reduce the oven temperature to 350°F (180°C). Bake the potatoes for 15 to 20 minutes.

SRIRACHA-LIME GRILLED CORN WITH QUESO FRESCO

And you thought herb butter was impressive. Until now. The garlicky-lime sriracha butter used here is the stuff dreams are made of. Hoard it for later to slather on cornbread, flank steak—even popcorn.

INGREDIENTS

SRIRACHA BUTTER

½ cup (115g/4oz) salted butter, at room temperature (1 stick)

¼ cup (60ml/2fl oz) sriracha

2 garlic cloves, minced

2 teaspoons lime zest (about 2 limes)

1 teaspoon sea salt

1 teaspoon freshly ground black pepper

4 ears corn, silks removed but husks left intact

½ cup (120ml/4fl oz) lime juice (about 4 limes)

½ cup (60g/2oz) queso fresco, crumbled

COOKING INSTRUCTIONS

1. Soak corncobs in their husks in cold water for at least 10 minutes, then drain.

2. To make the sriracha butter, combine the softened butter, sriracha, garlic, lime zest, salt, and pepper in a food processor and mix until smooth. This can be made in advance, covered, and kept in the refrigerator for up to one week.

3. Heat a grill or grill pan to high heat.

4. Place the soaked corn on the grill and close the lid. Cook, turning occasionally, for 15 to 20 minutes, or until steamed and cooked throughout.

5. Once tender, unwrap the husks and immediately spread with sriracha butter.

6. Drizzle with the lime juice and then sprinkle with queso. Serve immediately.

SUMMERTIME SUCCOTASH WITH BACON

Here's the best way to win over anyone who thinks they hate vegetables. Colorful, textured, and packed with all sorts of fantastic smoky-sweet heat, this baby is like nature's version of Skittles.

INGREDIENTS

¼ pound (115g) smoked bacon, diced (about 3 slices)

1 small sweet onion, diced

2 garlic cloves, minced

4 ears sweet corn, kernels only

1 jalapeño, seeded and minced

1 10-ounce package frozen lima beans, thawed

½ pound (225g) okra, cut into ½-inch (1.5cm) thick slices

1 pound (450g) grape tomatoes, halved

¼ cup (60ml/2fl oz) sriracha

2 tablespoons apple cider vinegar

1 teaspoon sea salt

1 teaspoon freshly ground black pepper

¼ cup (6g/¼oz) basil, chopped

COOKING INSTRUCTIONS

1. Cook the bacon in a large skillet over medium heat until crispy, about 5 to 7 minutes. Transfer with a slotted spoon to a paper towel–lined plate. Leave the bacon fat in the skillet.

2. Add the onion and garlic to the skillet and sauté, stirring occasionally, for 3 to 5 minutes, stirring occasionally, until the onion is soft and translucent.

3. Add the corn, jalapeño, lima beans, okra, and tomatoes. Cook until everything is tender, stirring constantly, about 5 minutes.

4. Stir in the sriracha, apple cider vinegar, salt, pepper, and basil.

5. Garnish with the crispy bacon and serve.

CHILI, GARLIC, AND GINGER SAUTÉED GREENS

Serves 4

Worst feeling ever: Spending tons on locally grown leafy things at the farmers' market, only to forget about them and wind up with a soggy brown mass. Keep this recipe handy to ensure a different fate.

INGREDIENTS

2 tablespoons sesame oil

2 tablespoons soy sauce

2 tablespoons sriracha

1 tablespoon fresh ginger root, peeled and minced

2 garlic cloves, minced

2 pounds (900g) tender greens (such as spinach, watercress, beet greens, baby kale, dandelion greens, or escarole), thick stems removed and leaves coarsely chopped

1 tablespoon toasted sesame seeds

COOKING INSTRUCTIONS

1. Heat the sesame oil in a large pot over medium heat.

2. While the oil is heating, combine the soy sauce, sriracha, ginger, and garlic in a small bowl and mix well.

3. Once the oil is hot, add the greens to the pot and cook, tossing occasionally, until wilted, about 3 to 4 minutes.

4. Add the sauce and cook for another 2 minutes, tossing occasionally.

5. Garnish with sesame seeds and serve.

SUPER-SPICED FALAFEL WITH TAHINI SAUCE

Makes 12 falafels

Finally, a dish to wow all those vegetarian friends of yours when they come over for dinner. Plus, it's filling and robust enough to satisfy diehard meatatarians, too.

INGREDIENTS

3 tablespoons olive oil, divided
1 small onion, diced
2 garlic cloves, minced
1 15-ounce can chickpeas, rinsed
    and drained
¼ cup (60ml/2fl oz) sriracha
¼ cup (15g/½oz) parsley, chopped
¼ cup (28g/1oz) panko
    (Japanese breadcrumbs)
2 teaspoons ground cumin
2 teaspoons ground coriander

1 teaspoon sea salt
1 large egg, lightly beaten

TAHINI SAUCE
1 cup (235ml/8fl oz) tahini
½ cup (120ml/4fl oz) sriracha
½ cup (120ml/4fl oz) water
½ cup (120ml/4fl oz) freshly squeezed
    lemon juice (about 3 lemons)
1 teaspoon sea salt

COOKING INSTRUCTIONS

1. Heat 1 tablespoon of olive oil in a large sauté pan over medium heat. Add the onion and garlic and sauté for 5 minutes, or until softened.

2. Combine the sautéed onion and garlic in a large bowl along with the chickpeas, sriracha, parsley, panko, cumin, coriander, and salt. Mash with a fork or potato masher until the chickpeas are broken down and mushy.

3. Add the beaten egg. Using your hands, mash until it all comes together.

4. Using wet hands, shape the mixture into twelve falafel balls and then flatten each ball with the palm of your hand.

5. In the same sauté pan, heat the remaining olive oil over medium-high heat. Fry the falafel for 3 minutes on each side.

6. While the falafel are cooking, make the tahini sauce. In a medium bowl, whisk together the tahini, sriracha, water, lemon juice, and salt until smooth and creamy.

7. Serve the hot falafel with the tahini sauce.

FOUR-ALARM BAKED MAC AND CHEESE

You know how decadently reckless it feels to spoon frosting from the bowl? Same applies here. Sometimes, you just need to skip the topping and baking and eat it straight up from the stovetop.

INGREDIENTS

Baking spray

1 pound (450g) elbow macaroni

4 cups, or 1 quart (950ml/32fl oz) milk

½ cup (120ml/4fl oz) sriracha

6 tablespoons (85g/3oz) unsalted butter, divided (¾ stick)

½ cup (60g/2oz) all-purpose flour

3 cups (230g/12oz) gruyère, grated

2 cups (225g/8oz) extra-sharp cheddar, grated

1 teaspoon sea salt

1 teaspoon freshly ground black pepper

½ teaspoon freshly grated nutmeg

PANKO TOPPING

2 tablespoons unsalted butter

2 tablespoons sriracha

1½ cups (170g/6oz) panko (Japanese breadcrumbs)

COOKING INSTRUCTIONS

1. Preheat the oven to 375°F (190°C). Spray a 9 x 13-inch (23 x 33cm) baking dish with baking spray and set aside.

2. Bring a large pot of salted water to a boil. Cook the macaroni according to package directions, or until al dente. Drain well.

3. Heat the milk and sriracha in a medium saucepan over medium heat until hot, but not boiling.

4. Melt the butter in a large saucepan over medium heat. Whisk in the flour, then reduce the heat to low and cook for 2 minutes, stirring constantly. While whisking, add the hot sriracha milk and cook, whisking constantly, for another 4 minutes, or until thickened and smooth.

Instructions continued on next page

FOUR-ALARM BAKED MAC AND CHEESE

Continue

COOKING INSTRUCTIONS

5. Remove from heat and whisk in the gruyère, cheddar, salt, pepper, and nutmeg. Stir until the cheese is melted.

6. Add the cooked macaroni to the sauce, stir to combine, and pour into the prepared baking dish.

7. To prepare the topping, melt the remaining 2 tablespoons butter in a medium sauté pan over medium heat. Once melted, add the sriracha and panko and stir to combine. Spread over the top of the mac and cheese.

8. Bake for 30 to 35 minutes, or until the sauce is bubbly and the top is crisp and golden.

DESSERTS

SIZZLING CHILI AND LIME DONUTS

So you love donuts but don't want to feel like a fatty for eating them. Bingo—these are baked donuts! While they don't have quite the same crumb as their fried counterpart, they're delightfully dense and chewy.

INGREDIENTS

Cooking spray, for greasing
1½ cups (190g/6 ¾oz) all-purpose flour
¾ cup (150g/5¼oz) sugar
1 teaspoon baking powder
½ teaspoon baking soda
¼ teaspoon kosher salt
1 large egg
⅝ cup (125g/5oz) plain Greek yogurt
⅓ cup (80ml/2¾fl oz) vegetable oil
¼ cup (60ml/2fl oz) whole milk

¼ cup (60ml/2fl oz) sriracha
2 tablespoons freshly squeezed lime juice (about 1 lime)
2 tablespoons lime zest (about 6 limes)

GLAZE
2 cups (200g/7oz) powdered sugar
½ cup (120ml/4fl oz) freshly squeezed lime juice (about 4 limes)
1 tablespoon lime zest (about 3 limes)

COOKING INSTRUCTIONS

1. Preheat the oven to 325°F (160°C). Lightly grease a donut pan with cooking spray.

2. In a medium bowl, whisk together the flour, sugar, baking powder, baking soda, and salt. Set aside.

3. In a large bowl, lightly beat the egg. Add the yogurt, vegetable oil, milk, sriracha, lime juice, and lime zest. Mix until well combined.

4. Gently stir the dry ingredients into the wet ingredients and mix until just incorporated.

5. Transfer the dough to a zip-tight plastic bag and cut off a corner to use as a piping bag. Pipe the dough into the greased donut pan, filling each cup about half full.

6. Bake for 10 to 12 minutes, or until the donut springs back when lightly touched.

7. Remove the donuts from the pan and allow to cool for 10 minutes. Repeat with the remaining dough.

8. To make the glaze, mix the powdered sugar, lime juice, and lime zest in a medium bowl. Dip the tops of the cooled donuts into the glaze and serve.

SRIRACHA PEANUT BUTTER CHOCOLATE CHIP COOKIES

> **Makes 54 cookies**

Like a good date, these babies are best with a little hands-on action. Rolling the dough through turbinado sugar (aka raw sugar) before baking is crucial to impart sweetness and a bit of texture.

INGREDIENTS

1 cup (225g/8oz) unsalted butter, at room temperature (2 sticks)

1½ cups (390ml/14oz) crunchy peanut butter

1 cup (200g/7oz) sugar

1 cup (220g/7¾oz) light brown sugar, tightly packed

¼ cup (60ml/2fl oz) sriracha

2 large eggs

1 teaspoon vanilla extract

3 cups (375g/13oz) all-purpose flour

1½ teaspoons baking soda

1 teaspoon baking powder

1 teaspoon sea salt

1½ cups (255g/9oz) semisweet chocolate chips

1 cup (200g/7oz) turbinado sugar

COOKING INSTRUCTIONS

1. Preheat the oven to 375°F (190°C). Line two large baking sheets with silpat or parchment paper and set aside.

2. In a large bowl, using a handheld mixer, cream the butter, peanut butter, sugar, and brown sugar on medium speed until the sugar dissolves and the mixture is light and fluffy, about 3 to 4 minutes.

3. Add the sriracha, eggs, and vanilla and blend for 1 minute, or until well incorporated.

4. In a medium bowl, whisk together the flour, baking soda, baking powder, and salt.

5. Add the dry ingredients to the wet ingredients and mix for 1 to 2 minutes on medium speed until well blended. Fold in the chocolate chips.

6. Place the turbinado sugar on a plate.

7. Using a 1½-tablespoon scoop, scoop the dough into balls and then roll them in the sugar. Arrange the dough 2 inches (5cm) apart on the prepared baking sheets and continue with the remaining dough.

8. Flatten the dough with a fork and make a crisscross pattern on each cookie.

9. Bake for 8 to 10 minutes, or until the cookies just begin to brown.

10. Cool on wire racks, and enjoy!

FIRESTARTER BLONDIES

Makes 12 blond[ies]

This recipe makes twelve blondies—or, as I like to call it, a weekend serving. They honestly won't last longer than that, as they're all kinds of cakey, buttery, and the right side of different.

INGREDIENTS

Cooking spray, for greasing
1 cup (125g/4½oz) all-purpose flour
½ teaspoon baking powder
⅛ teaspoon baking soda
½ teaspoon kosher salt
½ cup (115g/4oz) unsalted butter, melted (1 stick)
1 cup (220g/7¾oz) light brown sugar, packed
1 large egg
2 tablespoons sriracha
1 tablespoon vanilla extract
1 cup (170g/6oz) white chocolate chips

COOKING INSTRUCTIONS

1. Preheat the oven to 350°F (180°C). Grease an 8 x 8-inch (20 x 20cm) baking pan with cooking spray.

2. In a medium bowl, whisk together the flour, baking powder, baking soda, and salt. Set aside.

3. In a large bowl, stir together the melted butter and brown sugar. Add the egg, sriracha, and vanilla and mix well to combine.

4. Add the flour mixture to the butter mixture and stir until combined. Fold in the white chocolate chips.

5. Spread the batter into the prepared pan. Bake for 18 to 23 minutes, or until a toothpick inserted in the center comes out clean. For doughier brownies, bake closer to the 18-minute mark; if you prefer cake-like brownies, bake longer.

6. Cut into squares and serve.

SPICY CHOCOLATE CUPCAKES WITH CHILI-CHOCOLATE FROSTING

Makes 24 cupcakes

Similar to that demurely dressed friend who secretly hides her tramp stamp, these cupcakes aren't quite what they seem—chocolaty, sure, but also devilishly rich with a subtle, surprising heat on the finish.

INGREDIENTS

2¼ cups (280g/10oz) all-purpose flour

¾ cup (65g/2 ⅓oz) unsweetened cocoa powder

2¼ teaspoons baking powder

1½ teaspoons ground cinnamon

¾ teaspoon kosher salt

1 cup (235ml/8fl oz) whole milk

½ cup (120ml/4fl oz) sriracha

1½ teaspoons vanilla extract

½ cup (85g/3oz) semisweet chocolate chips

¾ cup (170g/6oz) unsalted butter, at room temperature (1½ sticks)

1 cup (200g/7oz) sugar

1 large egg

2 large egg yolks

CHILI-CHOCOLATE FROSTING

1½ cups (355ml/12fl oz) heavy cream

2 cups (340g/12oz) semisweet chocolate chips

¼ cup (60g/2oz) unsalted butter, at room temperature (½ stick)

1 tablespoon sriracha

2½ cups (300g/10½oz) powdered sugar

COOKING INSTRUCTIONS

1. Preheat the oven to 350°F (180°C). Line two muffin tins with cupcake liners and set aside.

2. In a large bowl, whisk together the flour, cocoa powder, baking powder, cinnamon, and salt. Set aside.

3. In a small bowl, combine the milk, sriracha, and vanilla and set aside.

4. In a small microwave-safe bowl, heat the chocolate chips in the microwave for 30-second intervals until melted, stirring and checking at each interval, about 1 to 2 minutes total.

5. In a large bowl, using a handheld mixer, beat the butter and sugar until light and fluffy, about 3 minutes. Stir in the melted chocolate and mix for an additional 1 minute, scraping down the sides.

Instructions continued on next page

SPICY CHOCOLATE CUPCAKES WITH CHILI-CHOCOLATE FROSTING

Continu

COOKING INSTRUCTIONS

6. Add the whole egg and egg yolks, beating until well combined, about 1 to 2 minutes.

7. With the mixer on low speed, add one-third of the flour mixture to the chocolate batter and mix to combine. Pour in one-third of the sriracha-milk mixture and mix to combine. Repeat until you have incorporated all of the flour and milk.

8. Scoop the batter into the cupcake liners, filling the cups about two-thirds full. Bake for 20 to 23 minutes, or until a toothpick inserted in the center of a cupcake comes out clean. Cool for 10 minutes in the pan and then transfer to a wire rack to cool completely.

9. To make the chili-chocolate frosting, heat the heavy cream in a medium pan over medium-low heat until just simmering, about 3 minutes. Remove the cream from the heat, add the chocolate chips, and stir until melted. Allow to cool for 10 minutes.

10. Add the butter and sriracha to the cream mixture and stir to combine. Let cool for another 20 minutes.

11. Mix in the powdered sugar, transfer the mixture to a bowl, cover with plastic wrap, and refrigerate for 1 hour.

12. Transfer the mixture to a large bowl and whip until the frosting is light and fluffy, about 1 to 3 minutes.

13. Pipe the frosting onto the cooled cupcakes and serve.

DRINKS

SRIRACHA BLOODY MARY

People who say they don't like a Bloody Mary are people who haven't had a good one. This version delivers. It's peppery and piquant and begging for you to host brunch already.

INGREDIENTS

1 32-ounce bottle tomato juice

½ cup (120ml/4fl oz) freshly squeezed lemon juice

2 cups (475ml/16fl oz) vodka

¾ cup (180ml/6fl oz) Worcestershire sauce

1 tablespoon salt

2 tablespoons pepper

2 tablespoons freshly grated horseradish

1 tablespoon dry mustard

½ cup (120ml/4fl oz) sriracha

Ice

Jackie O's Dark Apparition Imperial or a local stout beer, for topping off

GARNISHES*

Sriracha

Sea or kosher salt

Freshly ground black pepper

8 celery stalks

16 green olives

16 pickled haricot verts (optional)

16 pickled baby carrots (optional)

Toothpicks

*Have fun with these—use one or all! But don't skip on the spicy rim coated with sriracha, salt, and pepper.

INSTRUCTIONS

1. In a large pitcher, combine the tomato juice, lemon juice, vodka, Worcestershire sauce, salt, pepper, horseradish, dry mustard, and sriracha and stir vigorously.

2. When ready to serve the cocktails, rub or squirt sriracha around the rims of the serving glasses.

3. Combine the salt and pepper on a small plate and mix well. Dip the sriracha-rimmed glasses in the mixture to coat.

4. Fill each glass three-quarters with ice and then pour the pre-mixed Bloody Mary on top, topping the glass off with the stout beer.

5. Skewer olives or your favorite pickled veggies onto toothpicks. Garnish each glass with celery and veggie skewers and serve.

LYCHEE-LIME SPARKLER

Booze always makes things better, right? If there was one exception to that rule, this cocktail-mocktail is it. The limeade holds its own even without the vodka, making nice with guests of any age.

INGREDIENTS

1 20-ounce can lychees in syrup
1 cup (235ml/8fl oz) freshly squeezed lime juice (about 8 limes)
¼ cup (60ml/2fl oz) sriracha
½ teaspoon sea salt
2 cups (475ml/16fl oz) vodka or cold water
4 cups, or 1 quart (950ml/32fl oz) ice
4 slices lime

INSTRUCTIONS

1. In a blender, combine the lychees in their syrup, lime juice, sriracha, and salt. Blend on high until smooth, about 1 minute. Strain through a fine mesh strainer into a pitcher.

2. Add the vodka or water and whisk to combine. Add ice and serve in ice-filled glasses garnished with lime slices.

CERVEZA OF THE GODS

For us 99-percenters, jet-setting to the Mexican Riviera isn't happening anytime soon. But you might as well drink like it is! Here, any pale lager will do, so long as it's smooth, mild, and light.

INGREDIENTS

1 tablespoon sea salt
1 tablespoon chili powder
1 lime wedge

2 tablespoons tomato juice
1 tablespoon freshly squeezed lime juice
1½ tablespoons sriracha
Ice
12 ounces (355ml) pale Mexican beer, chilled
2 lime wedges

INSTRUCTIONS

1. Combine the salt and chili powder on a small plate. Moisten the rims of two pint glasses with the lime wedge and then dip the moistened rims into the salt mixture, turning to coat.

2. Combine the tomato juice, lime juice, and sriracha in a small bowl. Divide between the two glasses.

3. Add enough ice to fill each glass about two-thirds full.

4. Pour the beer into each glass, tipping the glass at an angle as you pour, and garnish with a lime wedge.

THAI FIRECRACKER

To keep this drink on its toes, make sure the champagne you use isn't too sweet; otherwise, you'll err on the side of syrupy-tasting. Opt for a dry champagne, crisp sparkling wine, or prosecco.

INGREDIENTS

2 ounces (60ml) dry gin
2 ounces (60ml) mango juice
2 ounces (60ml) cucumber water
1 tablespoon sriracha
Ice
1 ounce (30ml) champagne
1 lime wedge, for garnish

INSTRUCTIONS

1. In a cocktail shaker, combine the gin, mango juice, cucumber water, and sriracha with ice and shake. Strain into an ice-filled glass.

2. Top with champagne and serve with a lime wedge.

CINNAMON CITRUS FIREBALL

Serves 2

No one will see this cocktail coming. What looks to be a meek and mild mai tai is actually a bracing blow-the-doors-off-the-joint concoction of cinnamon-flavored whisky and bittersweet citrusy liqueur.

INGREDIENTS

Ice

3 ounces (90ml) rye whiskey

1 ounce (30ml) Fireball Whiskey

1 ounce (30ml) Aperol

¼ cup (60ml/2fl oz) freshly squeezed orange juice (less than 1 orange)

1 tablespoon sriracha

2 orange twists

INSTRUCTIONS

1. Fill a cocktail shaker with ice. Add rye, Fireball, Aperol, orange juice, and sriracha.

2. Shake for 15 seconds, then strain into an ice-filled old-fashioned glass and garnish with an orange twist.

HOT JIMMY

This revved-up cocktail comes on strong like a love affair. It's fizzy, bold, and full of surprises—just don't blame us if you're left shaking, sweaty and immediately wanting more.

INGREDIENTS

¼ teaspoon sriracha
1½ ounces (45ml) bourbon
2 ounces (60ml) cranberry juice
3 ounces (90ml) soda water
Jalapeño

INSTRUCTIONS

1. In a cocktail shaker, combine sriracha, bourbon, and cranberry juice and shake vigorously.

2. Pour into a highball glass and add soda water to fill.

3. Garnish with a jalapeño ring.

DILLISH THRILLER SHOT

Three ingredients; one wicked way to light your night on fire. This killer takes no prisoners, as the briny pickle juice cuts the vodka, leaving you with nothing but that sweet-hot heat.

INGREDIENTS

½ ounces (15ml) pepper vodka
2 ounces (60ml) pickle juice
⅛ teaspoon sriracha

INSTRUCTIONS

1. In a rocks glass, mix the vodka and pickle juice.

2. Place the sriracha on your hand in the hollow between the forefinger and thumb.

3. Lick sriracha off your hand and shoot the rocks glass.

SPICY GINGER-BASIL COCKTAIL

Serves 1

Those amateurs at the over-hyped salsa club can have their mojitos. This distinguished drink is less sweet and far more intriguing, offering up a bit of everything: herbaceous, honeyed, fiery, and fizzy.

INGREDIENTS

3 basil leaves, plus 1 basil sprig for garnish

4 drops sriracha, more or less to taste

2 ounces (60ml) good-quality ginger beer

2 ounces (60ml) vodka

Ice

INSTRUCTIONS

1.   In a rocks glass or cocktail shaker, muddle 3 basil leaves and the sriracha.

2.   Add the ginger beer, vodka, and ice. If using a rocks glass, swirl to combine and add the basil sprig for garnish. If using a cocktail shaker, toss back and forth two times, then pour into a collins glass and garnish with the basil sprig.

INDEX

About the Author

Melissa Petitto is a registered dietician, personal chef with an A-list clientele, and self-confessed sriracha addict. She custom designs menus for her clients and prepares meals for them with the freshest ingredients. Petitto has received the top honor of Apprentice Cuisinier at Johnson & Wales University and has worked in the test kitchen at *Cooking Light* magazine. Her other books include *An Apple A Day* and *30-Minute Paleo Meals.*

About the Contributing Mixologist

John Edwards Clift has been making cocktails around the Midwest since 1999. He enjoys the local craft beer and distilling scene and is currently the state ambassador for Jackie O's Brewery in Athens, Ohio. If he's not making cocktails, you can find John at any number of beer and spirit events or a good rock show.